Bibliographic information published by the German National Library:

The German National Library lists this publication in the National Bibliography; detailed bibliographic data are available on the Internet at http://dnb.dnb.de .

Imprint:

Copyright © 2018 GRIN Verlag
Print and binding: Books on Demand GmbH, Norderstedt Germany
ISBN: 9783668882997

This book at GRIN:

https://www.grin.com/document/459744

Charles Lustig

Bob Dylan's significance for the music industry based on the selected songs and focussing on the years 1965–1975

GRIN Verlag

GRIN - Your knowledge has value

Since its foundation in 1998, GRIN has specialized in publishing academic texts by students, college teachers and other academics as e-book and printed book. The website www.grin.com is an ideal platform for presenting term papers, final papers, scientific essays, dissertations and specialist books.

Visit us on the internet:

http://www.grin.com/

http://www.facebook.com/grincom

http://www.twitter.com/grin_com

Bob Dylan's significance for the music industry based on the selected songs and focussing on the years 1965 – 1975

Term paper for the english course

School year 2018/19

Table of Contents

Introduction

Bob Dylan has released thirty-eight studio albums, which, until today, have sold over 120 million copies around the world.[1]

On October 13, 2016, Dylan was awarded the Nobel Prize in Literature "for having created new poetic expressions within the great American song tradition".[2] Sara Danius, the Swedish Academy's permanent secretary, drew parallels between his work and that of ancient Greek poets and stated that Dylan "is a great poet in the English-speaking tradition".[3] Besides that, he has been awarded the French Legion of Honor, a Pulitzer Prize Special Citation, a doctorate from Scotland's University of St. Andrews, and the Presidential Medal of Freedom.[4] When Bruce Springsteen introduced Bob Dylan into the *Rock and Roll Hall of Fame* in 1988, he said: "When I was 15 and I heard 'Like a Rolling Stone,' I heard a guy who had the guts to take on the whole world and who made me feel like I had to too."[5]

This paper should provide a better view on the influence Bob Dylan had on the music industry, focusing on the years 1965 – 1975, while answering the questions of why he became an important figure in music. For this term paper, it's important that the reader listens to the two analyzed and described songs *Like a Rolling Stone from* from the album *Highway 61 Revisited* and *Tangled Up in Blue* from the album *Blood on the Tracks* at least once, to be able to comprehend the conclusions and thoughts. Furthermore it is not necessary to be familiar with technical terms, since they will all get described within the paper.

However, this term paper can only cover the most important facts in a compressed way, due to the maximal length of twelve pages. In addition, the two songs could only be analyzed briefly by picking out parts from the lyrics and covering the most important and interesting facts.

Nuances regarding the subject, such as other musicians, songs and genres Dylan had influence on between 1965 to 1975, as well as a detailed view on his other albums, had to be left out.

---

[1] Cf. Bob Dylan, 2017, The Nobel Lecture, p. 25.
[2] Laura Smith-Spark, 2016, Bob Dylan wins 2016 Nobel Prize for Literature.
[3] Laura Smith Spark, 2016.
[4] Bob Dylan, The Nobel Lecture, p. 25.
[5] Andy Greene, 2015, Bob Dylan Recorded 'Like a Rolling Stone' 50 Years Ago Today.

Biography of Bob Dylan

Bob Dylan, born as Robert Allen Zimmerman on May 24, 1941 in Duluth, Minnesota, is an American singer-songwriter who has been active in the music industry for more than five decades. Dylan's musical genres are considered to be folk, blues, rock, gospel, country and pop standards.[6]

His paternal grandparents emigrated from Odessa, Russia to the United States, while his maternal grandparents were Lithuanian Jews who emigrated to the United States in 1902.[7] Bob Dylan started making music and played in a band when he was in high school. In his Nobel Prize lecture, Dylan remembered that, at the age of 17, he went to a Buddy Holly concert and described that day as one of the most influental days regarding his career as a musician:

"He looked me right straight dead in the eye, and he transmitted something. Something I didn't know what. and it gave me the chills.".[8] Therefore Bob Dylan's first major influence, before be became a real musician, was Buddy Holly, just a few days before his plane crashed, known as *The Day the music died*.[9]

Influenced by blues and country music through radio stations in his youth, as well as folk singers like Dave Van Ronk and Fred Neil, Dylan started playing at small clubs around Greenwich Village.[10] While being able to play at different clubs during 1961, Dylan was able to befriend with the singer Carolyn Hester, which lead to a feature with Bob Dylan on her third Album.[11] Dylan caught the attention of the album's producer John Hammond, who signed him to Columbia Records. His self-titled Album has been released in 1962 at the age of 20.[12] However, the release of the 1963 album "The Freewheelin' Bob Dylan" has been considered as his breakthrough in the music industry. Through the years Bob Dylan would become known as a "protest" singer, due to songs like *Blowin' in the Wind* (1963), *The Times They Are a-Changin* (1964) and *Hurricane* (1976), although he never saw himself as a protest singer in any form.[13] After a motorcycle accident in 1966, that has been considered as very impactful in Dylans life, he refused to tour for eight years.[14] Influenced by politics, philosophy, social and literary, he would keep making music for more than six decades and has toured with his Band since the late 1980s on what has been dubbed as the *The Never*

---

[6] Cf. Mick gold, 2005, Bob Dylan.
[7] Cf. Mick gold.
[8] Bob Dylan, The Nobel Lecture, 2017, p. 2.
[9] Cf. History.com Editors, 2010, The day the music died.
[10] Cf. Mick gold.
[11] Cf. Mick Gold.
[12] Cf. Bruce Eder, 2016, Bob Dylan by Bob Dylan.
[13] Cf. Ben Corbett, 2017, Bob Dylan Timeline.
[14] Cf. Ben Corbett.

Ending Tour, followed by many awards and prizes. The magazine *Time 100* described him as an ''Master poet, caustic social critic and intrepid, guiding spirit oft he counterculture generation.''.[15]

Influence on the music industry before 1965

Bob Dylan was the name of Dylan's debut studio album, released on March 19, 1962 and published by Columbia Records. The album hasn't been considered a widely success and only sold 5,000 copies in the first year.[16] However, he already earned a reputation among other musicians as a strong songwriter and powerful talent, even when his first album only contained two original songs.[17] Then, one year later on January 13, 1963, Dylan released his album *The Freewheelin' Bob Dylan* with eleven out of thirteen original compositions. On this album, Dylan dealt with stories about the civil rights movements throughout the country, while also opening up on his anxiety about the fear of a nuclear warfare.[18] Especially because of this album, Dylan had been considered as a major artist, not only in the folk circuit, but as a musician in general.[19] In 1964, Dylan released *The Times They Are a-Changin*, his third studio album. It is an acoustic folk album with only his original compositions, that deals with racism, poverty and social change, but without so much of the humor from his previous album.[20] While the title track is one of Dylan's most famous songs, the album itself hasn't been marked as a big leap forward from *The Freewheelin' Bob Dylan* by fans and critics.[21]However many say that Dylan was able to capture the spirit of the social and political turmoil at this time.

Bob Dylan's fourth and last studio album before 1965 has been called *Another Side of Bob Dylan* and was released on August 8, 1964, just 7 month after his last album. Dylan changed his style with this album significantly; He moved away from his socially conscious style, which included a reflection of politics and civil rights movements, and wrote more graceful, poetic and layered tracks, such as *It Ain't Me Babe* and *Chimes Of Freedom.*[22] The music genre of the album was still considered as folk and Dylan wrote deeper and more personl lyrics than ever before, tried out more things with his instruments, e.g. using a piano to his

---

[15] Cf. Jay Cocks, 2014, Bob Dylan, the folk musician.
[16] Cf. Mick Gold, 2005, Bob Dylan.
[17] Cf. Todd Leopold, 2015, Bob Dylan, in the beginning.
[18] Cf. Mick Gold, 2008, The Freewheelin' Bob Dylan.
[19] Cf. Ben Corbett, 2017, Bob Dylan Timeline.
[20] Cf. DesolationRow, 2006, Bob Dylan: The Times They Are A-Changin'.
[21] Cf. Stephen Thomas Erlewine, 2016, The Times They Are A-Changin'.
[22] Cf. Stephen Thomas Erlewine, 2016, Another Side of Bob Dylan.

acoustic guitar and harmonica, and with his music overall, providing a steppingstone for his upcoming experimenting albums

Bringing It All Back Home and *Highway 61 Revisited* in 1965. Despite of the criticism for moving away from his old style, *Another Side of Bob Dylan* has been widely accepted, not just by his folk fans, but by the music industry overall.[23]

Analysing *Like a Rolling Stone*: The invention of folk rock

Highway 61 Revisited is Bob Dylan's sixth studio album and was released on August 30, 1965, 5 month after his last album *Bringing It All Back Home*. *Highway 61 Revisited* combined the two music genres folk rock and rock and roll. After Dylan's first experiments with electric instruments on the last album, Dylan hired for *Highway 61 Revisited* a full rock and roll band, including guitarist Michael Bloomfield.[24] The first track is called *Like a Rolling Stone*, a six minute long song that has been considered by the *Rolling Stone magazine* as the greatest song of all time: ''No other pop song has so thoroughly challenged and transformed the commercial laws and artistic conventions of its time, for all time.''[25]

To understand why this song gets praised so much, it is important to know its roots in the music genre. Folk music, in its earlierst form, includes traditional folk music, reaching back to the earliest times when humans began to make music in communities. In the 19th century europe, academics tried to preserve old traditional music by collecting ballads and notes that reach back as far as to the 16th century.[26] American folk music has no origin, can not be pinned down to one exact time or musician. Therefore, american folk music includes numerous music genres and contributed to the development of country, jazz, rock and roll and more. From early on, folk music has been from and for the people, without entertainment or profit purposes.[27] Then, in the 20th century, folk music experienced a revival, called the *American folk-music revival*, due to musicans like Woody Guthrie and Oscar Brand.[28] The revival had its peak in the 1960s, which lead to *folk rock*, a fusion of folk music and rock and roll, pushed forward by Bob Dylan and a band called *the Byrds*[29], who famously covered Dylan's *Mr. Tambourine Man*. This movement should have been a response to the musicians who came over from Britain, such as *the Beatles* and *the Who*, who had a big influence on the

---

[23] Cf. Stephen Thomas Erlewine, 2015, Another Side of Bob Dylan.
[24] Cf. Stephen Thomas Erlewine, 2015, Highway 61 Revisited.
[25] Rolling Stone Magazine, 2011, 500 Greatest Songs of All Time.
[26] Cf. Emma, 2018, History of Folk Music.
[27] Cf. Kim Ruehl, 2018, The History of American Folk Music.
[28] Cf. Kim Ruehl.
[29] Cf. Kim Ruehl, 2018, Folk Rock 101.

folk community.[30] Coming back to Bob Dylan's single *Like A Rolling Stone*, it was Dylan's first song that included rock and roll, together with electric instruments, stepping out of his iconic acoustic folk sound at this time and opening the door for him being a rock star.[31] Besides that, the Newport Folk Festival in 1965 has been marked as the day in which Dylan went officially electric. *Like A Rolling Stone* had been released five days earlier, which lead to an audience that had no idea what to expect and to one of the biggest controversies for Dylan himself.[32]

Electric Dylan controversy

Bob Dylan was 24 years old when he played at the Newport Folk Festival
on July 25, 1965 and for the first time, he had an electric guitar in his hands. He wanted to present a sample of new electric songs, some from his old album, some from the at this time upcoming album *Highway 61 Revisited*. The booing from the fans started when Dylan played the song *Maggie's Farm* from *Bringing It All Back Home*, but the situation got uncomfortable for him when he started playing *Like a Rolling Stone*, a mixture of booing and chants of ''Sellout!'' almost drowned the music.[33] Dylan saw nothing wrong with his music, especially because other musicians used electric instruments in the past.[34] While some people stated different reasons for why the fans were booing, for example due to bad sound quality and the short duration of the songs, some people were undeniably upset about the way Dylan played his songs.[35] The problems came with the expacations from his folk fans.

At this time, Dylan had a reputation as a protest singer and has been considered by some people as the *Voice of a generation*, a title, that he never liked:
''You feel like an impostor when someone thinks you're something and you're not.''[36] said Dylan in an interview. At this time, Dylan did what not a lot of other musicians did in the past, he changed his style completely and did not bother to have any excuses for this, especially because he always liked to experiment with his music. That's why the Newport Folk Festival was so important, Dylan pushed electric rock, combined with his poetry, more than anyone before and may have lost a lot of his once original folk fans, but gained a big group of rock and roll fans as well, which lead to all of his three albums from 1965 and 1966

---

[30] Cf. Kim Ruehl, Folk Rock 101.
[31] Cf. History Editors, 2009, Dylan goes electric at the Newport Folk Festival.
[32] Cf. History Editors.
[33] Cf. Ben Corbett, 2018, Bob Dylan Goes Electric.
[34] Cf. Ben Corbett.
[35] Cf. History Editors, Dylan goes electric at the Newport Folk Festival.
[36] Ed Bradley, 2004, Bob Dylan gives rare interview.

being in the Top Ten of the charts.[37] When Dylan played a concert on May 17, 1966, right before he started to play *Like a Rolling Stone*, someone in the audience shouted ''Judas!'', to which Dylan replied: ''I don't believe you, you're a liar.'', he turned around to his band and said ''Play fuckin' loud!''.[38]

Like a Rolling Stone was the song that pushed rock and roll into the public, connected folk with rock through a controversy and gave Bob Dylan a whole new audience, as well as a lot of respect for his lyrics and poetic expressions.

Redefining what can be said: A lyrical point-of-view

Like a Rolling Stone was not only a success for his sound, but also for his words. Dylan has been known for getting inspiration by other folk songs and artists from the past, but what made his tracks so great was the usage of words, rhymes and stories, or to put it in Dylan's words: ''What I did to break away was to take simple folk changes and put new imagery and attitude to them, use catchphrases and metaphor combined with a new set of ordinances that evolved into something different that had not been heard before.''[39]

At this time, music like folk, rock and pop, that was in the charts, did not cover a lot of subjects within the lyrics, most of them consisted of subjects like *love* or *nostalgia*, Dylan changed that.[40]

In case of *Like a Rolling Stone*, it tells the storie of a girl, named *Miss Lonely,* who went from riches to rags, as the opposite to *rags to riches*, which describes a persons rise from poverty to wealth, including some political undertones.

| *Once upon a time you dressed so fine*

| *You threw the bums a dime in your prime, didn't you?*

Miss Lonely had a good life, probably going to the best schools, having rich friends, and a carefree life. Besides that, the rhymes create a perfect flow when Dylan sings it, which again reflects her once flawless life.

| *Now you don't talk so loud*

| *Now you don't seem so proud*

| *About having to be scrounging for your next meal.*

---

[37] Cf. Richie Unterberger, 2010, Folk-Rock: An Overview.
[38] Cf. Uncut, 2005, Bob Dylan – Liket A Rolling Stone.
[39] Will Hermes, 2016, How Bob Dylan's 'Bringing It All Back Home' 'Stunned the World'.
[40] Cf. Will Hermes, 2016.

The crisis she has in her life leads to her downfall in society, which means that she has to survive in an unfamiliar world. Dylan does not sing this part as smooth as before, again reflection her circumstances.

| *How does it feel?*

| *To be without a home*

| *Like a complete unknown*

| *Like a rolling stone?*

Almost ironically, the narrator makes fun of *Miss Lonely* and enjoys that she lost everything and can do what ever she wants, since she is free in this world.

The song title also reffers to the sentence *A rolling stone gathers no moss,* inspired by Hank William's song *Lost Highway.*[41]

| *Nobody's ever taught ya' how to live on the street*

| *And now you're gonna have to get used to it*

Now she has to deal with reality and the harshness of experience. All the finest schools were not able to teach her how to survive in the real world.

| *With no direction home*

This verse is different than the other chorus and could describe the counterculture movement from the 1960s. Especially young people from this generation did not always knew what they wanted, but they knew they did not like the way things were and tried to find their way in this world, often through political activity.[42]

| *Ain't it hard when you discover that*

| *He really wasn't where it's at*

| *After he took from you everything he could steal.*

Mainly the younger generation at this time protest against war and for a peacful society. Dylan describes that politicans were just opportunists who pretend to care about the movements, just so they can steal everything they can from the people.

| *When ya' ain't got nothing, you got nothin' to lose*

| *You're invisible now, ya' got no secrets to conceal*

Since *Miss Lonely* was so materialistic and lost everything she owned, she does not need to be scared of anything anymore. *Miss Lonely* is at the level of the working class, or, even worse for her, at the same level as the people she once oppressed by her wealth, while ignoring and

---

Cf. Songfacts, 2016, Like a Rolling Stone.

Cf. Joyce Chepkemoi, 2018, What Was The Counterculture Of The 1960s and 1970s?.

making fun of them. Now she is just as inconsequential and invisible in this world. In the end, nobody cares about her anymore.

Like a Rolling Stone was one of Dylan's most daring songs. The different music elements, Dylan's youthfulness, the cynical sound in Dylan's voice and the lyrics make this song to one of the most important songs in music history, marking a shift in rock and roll and popular music. In 2014, Dylan's handwritten lyrics to *Like a Rolling Stone* fetched $2 million at an auction, a world record for a popular music manuscript.[43]

Nevertheless there has been one album, that has been considered as one of Dylan's best.

Tangled Up in Blue from Blood on the Tracks: Decoding a Bob Dylan song

Blood on the Tacks is seen by many as one of the best albums in Bob Dylan's career[44]

and a lot of Bob Dylan's future albums have been considered as "his best" since

Blood on the Tracks.[45] It has been released on January 20, 1975[46], 9 years after Dylan's impactful motorcycle accident, which lead to a change in song writing for him.[47]

In 1974, Dylan lived alone in New York and studied with Norman Raeben, a russian born painter and philosopher. Raeben not only changed Dylan's philosophy, but also the way how he writes his songs.[48]

Tangled Up in a Blue can be seen as a love song. The narrator describes his long lasting relationship, which eventually has fallen apart. Furthermore, it tells the journey of the narrator who tries to get his love back. Dylan's use of time in this song is part of what makes it so extraordinary, compared to his past work. Norman Raeben had a profound impact on how Dylan saw the world. That showed by how Dylan tried to write "time" in his songs. In the liner notes from *Biograph* (video notes about the composition of *Tangled Up in Blue*), Dylan explained in which direction he wanted to go:

"I was just trying to make it like a painting where you can see the different parts but then you can also see the whole of it."[49]

This can already be seen at the first verse of the song:

---

[43] Cf. Jon Blistein, 2014, Bob Dylan's 'Like a Rolling Stone' Lyrics Sell for $2 Million.
[44] Cf. Rolling Stone, 2012, Readers' Poll: The Best Bob Dylan Albums of All Time.
[45] Cf. Jody Rosen, 2006, Bob Dylan's Make-Out Album.
[46] Cf. Mick gold, 2018, Tangled up in Blue.
[47] Cf. Ben Corbett, 2018, Understanding the Impact of Bob Dylan's Motorcycle Accident.
[48] Cf. Bert Cartwright, 2019, Bob Dylan painting with Norman Raeben.
[49] Kevin Holmes, 2018, Why Bob Dylan's 'Tangled Up in Blue' is a Modern Masterpiece.

| *Early one morning the sun was shining*
| *I was laying in bed*
| *Wondering if she'd changed at all*
| *If her hair was still red*
| *Her folks they said our lives together*
| *Sure was going to be rough*
| *They never did like Mama's homemade dress*
| *Papa's bank book wasn't big enough*

The opening of the song begins with what feels like the **present** day, but it is referred to in the past tense. Then, the narrator jumps to a memory from the **past**, just to predict a rough **future**, based on these memories. The narrator constantly changes the tense, jumping from the present to a memory to the future.[50] Putting yesterday, today and tomorrow, all in the same room.

| *And I was standing on the side of the road*
| *Rain falling on my shoes*
| *Heading out for the East Coast*
| *Lord knows I've paid some dues*
| *Gettin' through*
| *Tangled up in blue.*

The narrator now tries to get his love back, written in past tense. He is looking at the **past**, but is not afraid of the future either. It marks the end of the relationship, but at the same time the narrator is looking at a possible new beginning with his love.

In 2018, Bob Dylan released *The Bootleg Series Vol. 14: More Blood, More Tracks*, including different version from *Tangled Up in Blue*.[51] In his career, Dylan worked a lot on the music of this song and he created different versions of the song since its release, leaving out different verses and singing it a different way.[52] Listening to a version of *Tangled Up in Blue* from *The Bootleg Series Vol. 14: More Blood, More Tracks,* for example *Tangled Up in Blue – Take 3, Remake 3*[53], it is getting obvious that Dylan sings the final version of *Tangled Up in Blue*, as it can be heard on the official album *Blood on the Tracks,* with much higher vocals.

---

[50] Cf. Kevin Holmes, 2018, Why Bob Dylan's 'Tangled Up in Blue' is a Modern Masterpiece.
[51] Cf. Ss112, 2018, The Bootleg Series Vol. 14: More Blood, More Tracks.
[52] Cf. Eleanor Barkhorn, 2005, Untangling ''Tanged Up in Blue''.
[53] Cf. Ss112, 2018.

| *She turned around to look at me*
| *As I was walking away*
| *I heard her say over my shoulder*
| *"We'll meet again someday on the avenue"*
| *Tangled up in blue.*

It sounds like Dylan is straining a lot, just to reach the notes of the song, which reflects perfectly the narrators desperate journey to get his love back.

The track is made up of seven verses, plus one instrumental passage including Dylan's harmonica.

The first two verses can be seen as summaries of the relationship while the last two, including Dylan's harmonica, present the narrators almost euphoric present or future journey to get his love back. The middle four verses provide a detailing view on the happenings in the narrator's life, describing the happenings for ''he'' and ''she''.[54]

Verse three and six are broad summaries of the events in the narrator's life, while four and five focus on clear and detailed situations in his life. Even when the narrator tells different stories and happenings throughout the song, his motivation is always his love. Dylan reminds us of that at the beginning, as well as at the tale end of the third verse and in the last verse:

| *So now I'm going back again*
| *I got to get her somehow*

In the fourth verse of the song, the narrator is meeting a woman, but we do not know if this is the woman he is trying to get back, or if this is another woman.

| *I muttered something underneath my breath*
| *She studied the lines on my face*
| *I must admit I felt a little uneasy*
| *When she bent down to tie the laces*
| *Of my shoe*
| *Tangled up in blue*

Considering that the narrator said before that the woman he meets is working in a topless place, together with the wordplay, could imply a sexual relationship. However, the penultimate line could be a symbol for her helping the narrator, or even Dylan himself, to get back on his feet. Dylan tries to put the listener in the narrator's shoes, so he feels just as confused and uncertain as the narrator himself.

---

[54] Cf. Eleanor Berkhorn, 2005, Untangling ''Tanged Up in Blue''.

| *She lit a burner on the stove and offered me a pipe*
| *"I thought you'd never say hello" she said*
| *"You look like the silent type"*
| *Then she opened up a book of poems*
| *And handed it to me*
| *Written by an Italian poet*
| *From the thirteenth century*

There has been a lot of speculation about what this book could be, but the timeline and themes match up with *Dante's Vita Nuova*[55], a book about Dantes feelings towards his love Beatrice. It's a collection of sonnets, one ballata and canzones,[56] all elevating Dantes love for Beatrice into something sacred.

When the narrator reads the book, Dylan's tone shifts for the rest of the verse, giving it a more personal tone:

| *And every one of them words rang true*
| *And glowed like burning coal*
| *Pouring off of every page*
| *Like it was written in my soul, from me to you*
| *Tangled up in blue*

Now, with no idea what to do, the narrator walks on, not knowing where he is heading to. He reflects on all the people who had an influence on him, officially leaving his past behind, now ready to get his love back. He and his love are both realizing that they were always destined for the same end point, they just had to take their own path to get there.

| *But me I'm still on the road*
| *Heading for another joint*
| *We always did feel the same*
| *We just saw it from a different point of view*
| *Tangled up in Blue*

Tangled Up in Blue tells a love story that has been told a million times. What makes it special, however, is the precision in the details, which Dylan is able to provide. There is nothing trivial, every line and every verse is well thought of. The timestamps in this song mimics our own memories, how they always go back and forth. With *Tangled Up in Blue*, Dylan takes the listener to his personal journey through the song, pulling and seeing his own meaning in this.

---

[55] Cf. Subho, 2018, Tangled Up in Blue: A Closer Look
[56] Cf. The Editors of Encyclopaedia Britannica, La vita nuova

Some say that it is the story of Dylan and his wife Sara[57], while other think it is a view on America's transition from the optimism of the 1960s to the melancholy of the 70s. Dylan always continued to change the song, played different versions in different cities, shifted lyrics and added new verses entirely.[58]

With *Tangled Up in Blue*, Bob Dylan created something unique and timeless, something, the listener can relate to and understand, on a very personal dimension.

Conclusions

Like a Rolling Stone marked the beginning of a new direction for Dylan. He went officially electric and was able to take regular folk music, combined it with rock and roll elements and created a whole new music genre; folk rock, while also being able to push rock and roll into the public. Together with his rhymes, word plays and the shift from typical subjects in songs like ''love'' and ''nostalgia'', into more serious ones like ''resentment'', *Like a Rolling Stone* is one of the most influental songs ever written in the music industry. Almost ten years after, Dylan presented with *Tangled Up in Blue* a typical love story, heard and seen over and over again in the music and film industry, but with a big twist. His play with time, usage of words, meticulous details and way of story telling made this song to one of Dylan's most insightful.

Taking all this things into account, while keeping in mind that *Like a Rolling Stone* and *Tangled Up in Blue* are just two songs out of hundred Dylan wrote between 1965 -1975, there is no question about how significant and remarkable these songs truely are. Bob Dylan is, without a doubt, one of the most influental poets and music artists of the 20th century, if not of all time, who influenced and inspired hundred of other musicians since his first album and we are just starting to understand how important his songs, as a work of art, are.

---

[57] Cf. Kevin Holmes, 2018, Why Bob Dylan's 'Tangled Up in Blue' is a Modern Masterpiece.
[58] Cf. Eleanor Berkhorn, 2005, Untangling ''Tanged Up in Blue''.

Bibliography

Dylan, Bob: The Nobel Lecture, New York/United States 2017

Dylan, Bob: Chronicles (Volume One), Great Britain 2005

Wilentz, Sean: Dylan in America, London/Great Britain 2011

Hermes, Will(2016): How Bob Dylan's 'Bringing It All Back Home' 'Stunned the World'.

https://www.rollingstone.com/music/music-news/how-bob-dylans-bringing-it-all-back-home-stunned-the-world-158316/ 21.02.2018 23:38 Uhr

Landau, Jon(1975): Blood On The Tracks.

https://www.rollingstone.com/music/music-album-reviews/blood-on-the-tracks-255430/ 07.01.2018 18:23 Uhr

Kornhaber, Spencer(2017): Bob Dylan's Nobel Lecture says the unsayable.

https://www.theatlantic.com/entertainment/archive/2017/06/bob-dylan-nobel-literature-lecture-moby-dick-explanation/529284/ 21.02.2018 00:22 Uhr

Leopold, Todd(2015): Bob Dylan, in the beginning.

https://edition.cnn.com/2015/10/15/entertainment/gallery/tbt-bob-dylan/index.html 04.02.2018 00:12 Uhr

Ostalocutanje(2018): Folk rock.

https://en.wikipedia.org/wiki/Folk_rock 23.02.2018 17:28 Uhr

Jasper, Jay(2018): Tangled Up in Blue.

https://en.wikipedia.org/wiki/Tangled_Up_in_Blue 02.01.2018 18:32 Uhr

Gold, Mick(2018): Blood on the Tracks.

https://en.wikipedia.org/wiki/Blood_on_the_Tracks 02.01.2018 18:55 Uhr

Gold, Mick(2018): Bob Dylan.

https://en.wikipedia.org/wiki/Bob_Dylan#Going_electric 23.02.2018 17:34 Uhr

Pareles, Jon(2005): the Contrarian of a Generation, Revisited.

https://www.nytimes.com/2005/08/30/arts/music/the-contrarian-of-a-generation-revisited.html 09.01.2018 17:59 Uhr

Ss112(2018): The Bootleg Series Vol. 14: More Blood, More Tracks.

https://en.wikipedia.org/wiki/The_Bootleg_Series_Vol._14:_More_Blood,_More_Tracks 04.01.2018 13:23 Uhr

Smith-Park, Laura(2016): Bob Dylan wins 2016 Nobel Prize for Literature.

https://edition.cnn.com/2016/10/13/world/nobel-prize-literature/ 30.01.2018

Burling, Klas (1966/2018): Bob Dylan – Interview with Klas Burling.

https://y-fine.com/bob-dylan-interview/ 04.02.2018 15:04 Uhr

Gold, Mick(2008): The Freewheelin' Bob Dylan.

https://en.wikipedia.org/wiki/The_Freewheelin%27_Bob_Dylan 04.02.2018 15:34 Uhr

DesolationRow(2006): Bob Dylan, The Times They Are A-Changin'.

https://www.sputnikmusic.com/review/6131/Bob-Dylan-The-Times-They-Are-A-Changin/ 05.02.2018 22:22 Uhr

Hentoff, Nat(1964): Bob Dylan, The Wanderer.

https://www.newyorker.com/magazine/1964/10/24/the-crackin-shakin-breakin-sounds?CNDID=32655531&spMailingID=8567319&spUserID=MTA5MjQwODE2NTIwS0&spJobID=861962414&spReportId=ODYxOTYyNDE0S0 05.02.2018 22:41 Uhr

Erlewine, Stephen Thomas(2015): Another Side of Bob Dylan.

https://www.allmusic.com/album/another-side-of-bob-dylan-mw0000653105 05.02.2018 22:55 Uhr

Erlewine, Stephen Thomas(2015): Highway 61 Revisited.

https://www.allmusic.com/album/highway-61-revisited-mw0000189730 05.02.2018 00:55 Uhr

Rolling Stone(2011): 500 Greatest Songs of All Time.

https://www.rollingstone.com/music/music-lists/500-greatest-songs-of-all-time-151127/weezer-buddy-holly-71418/ 05.02.2018 23:28 Uhr

Erlewine, Stephen Thomas(2016): The Times They Are A-Changin'.

https://www.allmusic.com/album/the-times-they-are-a-changin-mw0000202344   11.02.2018 01:54 Uhr

Rolling   Stone(2010):   100   Greatest   Singers   of   All   Time.
https://www.rollingstone.com/music/music-lists/100-greatest-singers-of-all-time-147019/bob-dylan-29-226832/ 05.02.2018 23:54 Uhr

Kohl, Jerome(2008): Folk music.

https://en.wikipedia.org/wiki/Folk_music#19th-century_Europe 05.02.2018 23:39 Uhr

Ruehl, Kim(2018): The History of American Folk Music.

https://www.thoughtco.com/the-history-of-american-folk-music-1322572 05.02.2018 00:02 Uhr

Emma(2018): History of Folk Music.

https://ricketymusic.com/history-of-folk-music/ 02.02.2018 19:23 Uhr

Ruehl, Kim(2018): Folk Rock 101.

https://www.thoughtco.com/folk-rock-101-1322485 02.02.2018 19:50 Uhr

Uncut(2005): Bob Dylan – Like A Rolling Stone.

https://www.uncut.co.uk/features/bob-dylan-like-a-rolling-stone-44089

02.02.2018 20:44 Uhr

History Editors(2009): Dylan goes electric at the Newport Folk Festival.

https://www.history.com/this-day-in-history/dylan-goes-electric-at-the-newport-folk-festival

06.02.2018 22:39 Uhr

Corbett, Ben(2018): Bob Dylan Goes Electric.

https://www.thoughtco.com/bob-dylan-goes-electric-1322016 06.02.2018 22:47 Uhr

Bradley, Ed(2004): Bob Dylan gives rare Interview.

https://www.cbsnews.com/news/60-minutes-bob-dylan-rare-interview-2004/   02.02.2018

00:02 Uhr

Unterberger, Richie(2010): Folk-Rock: An Overview.

http://www.richieunterberger.com/turnover.html 02.02.2018 00:28 Uhr

Songfacts(2016): Like a Rolling Stone.

https://www.songfacts.com/facts/bob-dylan/like-a-rolling-stone 01.02.2018 19:44 Uhr

Greene, Andy(2015): Bob Dylan Recorded 'Like a Rolling Stone 50 Years Ago Today.

https://www.rollingstone.com/music/music-news/bob-dylan-recorded-like-a-rolling-stone-50-

years-ago-today-65422/ 01.02.2018 20:29 Uhr

Rosen, Jody(2006): Bob Dylan's Make-Out Album.

https://slate.com/culture/2006/08/bob-dylan-s-spectacular-new-album-modern-times.html

02.02.2018 19:22 Uhr

Chepkemoi, Joyce(2018): What Was The Counterculture Of The 1960s and 1970s?

https://www.worldatlas.com/articles/what-was-the-counterculture-of-the-1960s-and-70s.html

10.02.2018 20:23 Uhr

Murphy, Lily(2015): 50 years on, how does it feel?

http://www.themontrealreview.com/2009/Bob-Dylan-Like-a-Rolling-Stone.php   10.02.2018

23:29 Uhr

Blistein, Jon(2014): Bob Dylan's 'Like a Rolling Stone' Lyrics Sell for $2 Million.

https://www.rollingstone.com/music/music-news/bob-dylans-like-a-rolling-stone-lyrics-sell-

for-2-million-72332/ 10.02.2018 23:49 Uhr

Rolling Stone(2012): Readers' Poll: The Best Bob Dylan Albums of All Time.

https://www.rollingstone.com/music/music-lists/readers-poll-the-best-bob-dylan-albums-of-

all-time-12405/10-john-wesley-harding-64617/ 10.02.2018 23:55 Uhr

Gold, Mick(2005): Bob Dylan.

https://en.wikipedia.org/wiki/Bob_Dylan 10.02.2018 23:56 Uhr

Eder, Bruce(2016): Bob Dylan by Bob Dylan.

https://www.allmusic.com/album/bob-dylan-mw0000205218 10.02.2018 23:59 Uhr

Cocks, Jay(2014): Bob Dylan, the folk musician.

http://www.shrout.co.uk/TIME%20Bob%20Dylan.html 11.02.2018 1:24 Uhr

y2karl(2003): The Mysterious Norman Raeben.

https://www.metafilter.com/22787/The-Mysterious-Norman-Raeben

11.02.2018 2:22 Uhr

Corbett, Ben(2018): Understanding the Impact of Bob Dylan's Motorcycle Accident.

https://www.thoughtco.com/bob-dylans-motorcycle-accident-1322021

11.02.2018 3:02 Uhr

Cartwright, Bert(2019): Bob Dylan painting with Norman Raeben.

http://robertwaifegallery.com/ten-commandments-of-art/bob-dylan-and-painting-with-norman-raeben/ 11.02.2018 10:23 Uhr

Holmes, Kevin(2018): Why Bob Dylan's 'Tangled Up in Blue' is a Modern Masterpiece.

https://www.rockarchive.com/news/2018/bob-dylan-tangled-up-in-blue   11.02.2018   21:23 Uhr

Barkhorn, Eleanor(2005): Untangling ''Tangled Up in Blue''.

http://nassauweekly.com/untangling_tanged_up_in_blue/ 11.02.2018 22:34 Uhr

History.com Editors(2010): The day the music died.

https://www.history.com/this-day-in-history/the-day-the-music-died

11.02.2018 22:50 Uhr

Shubho(2018): Tangled Up in Blue: A Closer Look.

https://medium.com/@Ishubho/tangled-up-in-blue-a-closer-look-4581ac9df8a0

11.02.2018 22:23 Uhr

The Editors of Encyclopedia Britannica: La vita nuova.

https://www.britannica.com/topic/La-Vita-nuova 11.02.2018 23:45 Uhr

Attachment

Like a Rolling Stone, Highway 61 Revisited
By Bob Dylan, Produced by Tom Wilson

Tangled Up in Blue, Blood on the Tracks
By Bob Dylan, produced by Bob Dylan

Lyrics removed due to copyright issues

YOUR KNOWLEDGE HAS VALUE

- We will publish your bachelor's and
  master's thesis, essays and papers

- Your own eBook and book -
  sold worldwide in all relevant shops

- Earn money with each sale

Upload your text at www.GRIN.com
and publish for free